PROGRESSIVE

HOW TO TUNE THE GUITAR

by

Brett Duncan

Visit our Website
www.learntoplaymusic.com

The Progressive Series of Music Instruction Books, CDs, Videos and DVDs

CONTENTS

INTRODUCTION

Progressive How to Tune the Guitar contains a wealth of information to assist with the tuning of the guitar. Guitar players of all levels will find this book useful as it covers both simple tuning methods and advanced tuning methods. The accompanying CD will prove to be an invaluable aid to tuning the guitar as it contains many recordings of tuning notes. Throughout this book you will be introduced to some of the following points:

1. How to choose the right guitar for you and learn the parts of the guitar.
2. The different types of strings available and how to fit the strings to your guitar.
3. Useful setup and maintenance tips for the guitar to help keep your guitar in tune.
4. How to tune the guitar using a variety of methods such as using an electronic tuner, tuning the guitar to itself, tuning with harmonics, etc.
5. How to read guitar tablature and the basics of music notation for guitar.

A chord chart showing all the important basic chords has been included, as well as many examples of different playing styles.

For information on the *Progressive* series contact;
L.T.P. Publishing Pty Ltd
email: info@learntoplaymusic.com
or visit our website;
www.learntoplaymusic.com

USING THE COMPACT DISC

It is recommended that you have a copy of the accompanying compact disc that contains many tuning samples and a selection of previews of different music styles. Each tuning sample contains a note played several times. A separate track has been allocated to each tuning note giving you the option of setting your CD player to repeat that track as many times as you wish. Also recorded onto the CD are a collection of music pieces covering a variety of guitar styles. These tracks will give you an interesting insight into the many ways a guitar can be played. Throughout the book each tuning sample and music example is accompanied with a small picture of a compact disc and a number indicating the CD track number.   **12** ← CD Track Number

CHOOSING THE RIGHT GUITAR FOR YOU

Before purchasing a guitar there a several things to take into consideration. The main points are outlined below.

WHICH TYPE OF GUITAR?

There are basically four different types of guitar available, the **NYLON STRING GUITAR**, the **STEEL STRING ACOUSTIC GUITAR**, the **SOLID BODY ELECTRIC GUITAR** and the **HOLLOW BODY ELECTRIC GUITAR**. These guitars are discussed in detail over the following pages.

A nylon string guitar is mainly used in Classical and Flamenco styles.

A steel string guitar is mainly used in Folk, Country, Pop, Acoustic Rock and Traditional Blues styles.

A solid body electric guitar is mainly used in Rock, Modern Blues, Metal, Pop and Country Rock styles.

A hollow body electric guitar may be used for Rock, Pop etc. but is favoured for use in Jazz styles.

HOW MUCH TO SPEND?

The price of a guitar varies dramatically with many factors determining the quality and therefore the price of a guitar. Where it is made, how it is made, the materials that are used etc. For your first guitar it is not necessary to spend very much. Most beginning budget guitars are quite well made and will certainly suffice for the first 6 - 12 months of your learning. A budget priced beginning nylon string is often recommended as your first guitar to learn on. This type of guitar is often the cheapest and the easiest to play at first. After the initial learning period of 6 - 12 months you will be able to upgrade to either a better quality nylon string guitar or change to a steel string or electric guitar depending on which style you would like to concentrate on. Different guitar types and styles will be discussed in detail throughout the following sections.

FRETBOARD DIAGRAMS

Throughout the book several fretboard diagrams are used to highlight either an open string or a fretted note. A fretboard diagram is a grid of horizontal and vertical lines representing the strings and frets of the fretboard. An open circle represents an open string and a full black circle represents a fretted note. The number refers to the left hand finger which frets the note.

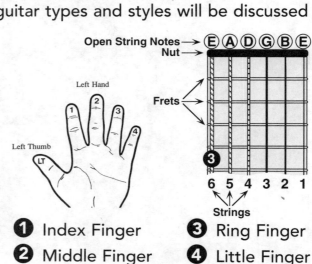

Open String Notes → Ⓔ Ⓐ Ⓓ Ⓖ Ⓑ Ⓔ
Nut →

Left Hand

Frets →

Left Thumb
LT

6 5 4 3 2 1
Strings

❶ Index Finger   **❸** Ring Finger
❷ Middle Finger   **❹** Little Finger

THE NYLON STRING GUITAR

The **NYLON** guitar has a wider neck than the other types of guitar. It is most commonly used for playing Classical, Flamenco and Fingerstyles. Generally it is much cheaper than other types of guitar and is recommended for beginning guitarists.

PARTS OF THE NYLON STRING GUITAR

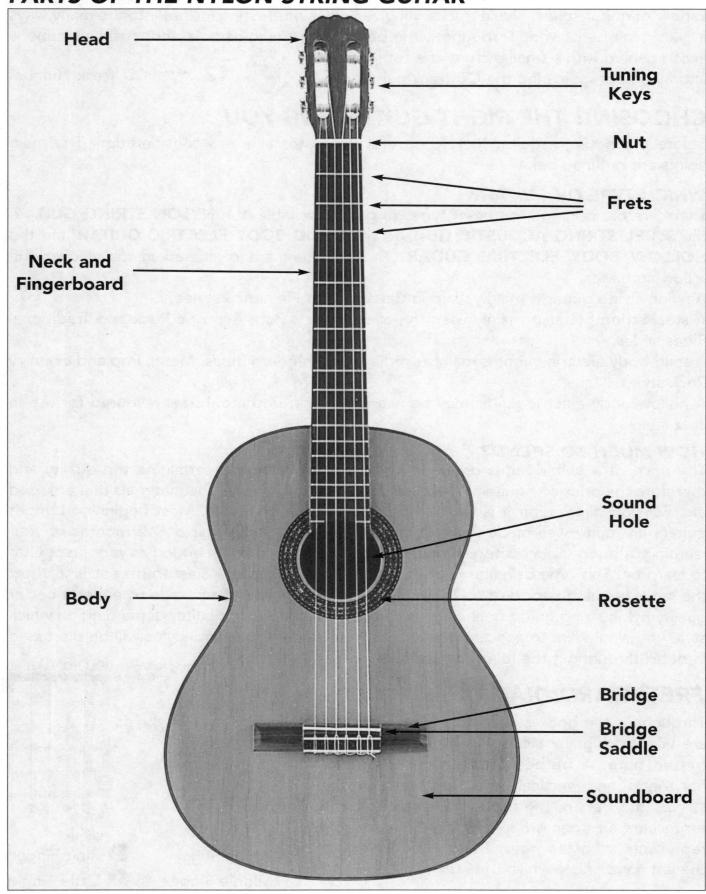

Head

Tuning Keys

Nut

Frets

Neck and Fingerboard

Sound Hole

Body

Rosette

Bridge

Bridge Saddle

Soundboard

NYLON STRING GUITAR SETUP
NYLON STRINGS

A nylon string guitar is fitted with three unwound strings (strings 1-3) and three wound strings (strings 4 - 6). It is important to have the correct set of strings fitted to your guitar, especially if you are a beginner.

There are basically three types of strings available for the nylon string guitar, high, normal and low tension strings. Until you build enough strength in your hands to fret the chords cleanly, low tension nylon strings are recommended. A reputable music store which sells guitar strings should be able to assist with this. Do not put steel strings on a nylon string guitar or it will damage the neck of the guitar.

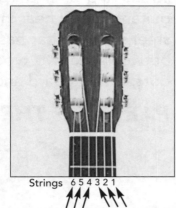

Strings 6 5 4 3 2 1

Steel Wound onto Nylon Strings   Plain Unwound Nylon Strings

FITTING NYLON STRINGS

Strings must be correctly fitted to the guitar otherwise you will encounter tuning problems. In the early stages of learning the guitar it is recommended that you get a qualified guitar repairer or an experienced guitar player to fit the strings to your guitar.

Tying the string to the bridge: There are basically two methods to tying the string to the bridge of a nylon string guitar. Study the following diagrams. With both types of knot shown it is important to finish the knot behind the back of the bridge. This will reduce the possibility of the string slipping.

Option 1.

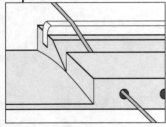 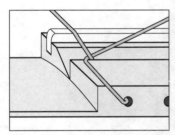 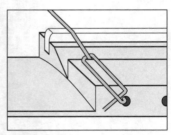

Step 1.   *Step 2.*   *Step 3.*

Option 2.

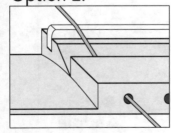 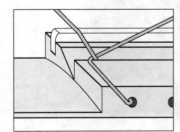 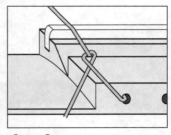 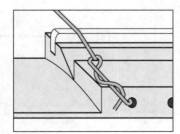

Step 1.   *Step 2.*   *Step 3.*   *Step 4.*

Tying the string to the tuning key:

It is important to have a short length of the string protruding through the hole in the tuning key barrel. This part of the string can then be clamped to the barrel as the string is coiled onto the barrel. See the adjacent diagram. The string should coil neatly around the barrel at least 4 - 5 times.

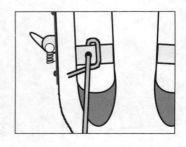 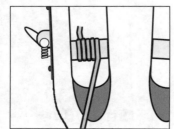

THE STEEL STRING GUITAR

The **STEEL STRING ACOUSTIC** has steel strings and is most commonly played by strumming or fingerpicking groups of notes called chords. This is the type of acoustic guitar you will hear in most modern styles of music e.g. Top 40 Rock and Pop music. The steel string guitar has a different shape than a classical guitar. Other notable differences between the two types of acoustic guitars is that most steel string guitars have position dots, a pick guard and a strap pin.

PARTS OF THE STEEL STRING GUITAR

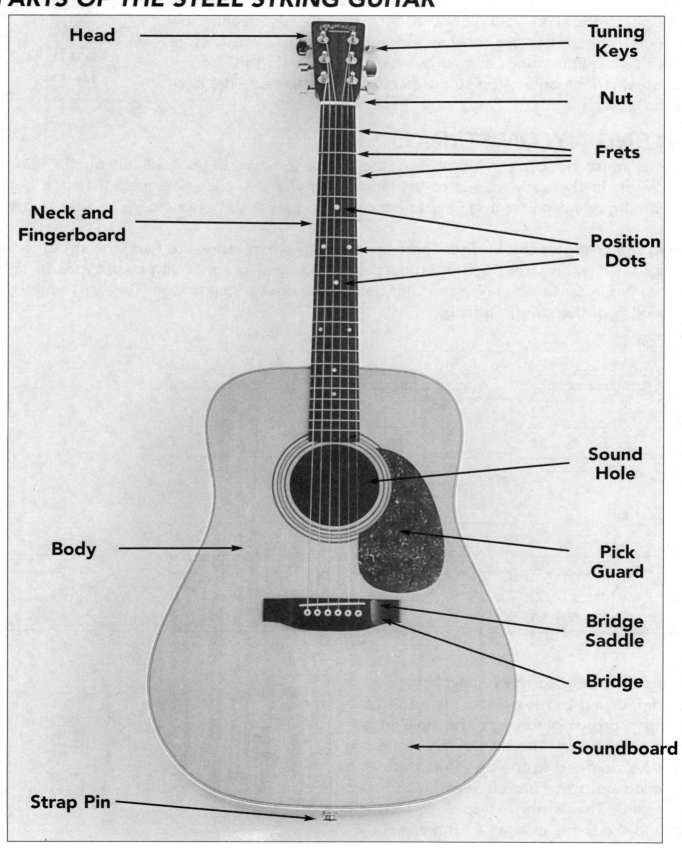

Head — Tuning Keys — Nut — Frets — Neck and Fingerboard — Position Dots — Sound Hole — Body — Pick Guard — Bridge Saddle — Bridge — Soundboard — Strap Pin

STEEL STRING GUITAR SETUP
STEEL STRINGS

There are many types of steel strings available. Steel strings come in a variety of gauges, different types of winding and can also be manufactured from different types of metal.

Steel string gauges vary from extra light to heavy. If you are learning on a steel string guitar then a light gauge or an extra light gauge is recommended. Almost all steel string guitars have two unwound strings (strings 1 and 2) and four wound strings (strings 3 - 6). The wound strings contain an inner core and an outer core. The main two types of wound strings are roundwound and flatwound. The roundwound strings are the most popular, made up of a round wire coiled around an inner steel core producing a definite coiled string. This type of string gives a strong, rich and loud sound. Flatwound strings use a strip winding to give a smooth feel to the string. This type of string produces a softer more mellow sound and as this type of string is easier on the fingers can be recommended for beginning guitarists. The most common material used for the wound steel strings is Bronze though Nickel, Brass and even Stainless Steel strings are available.

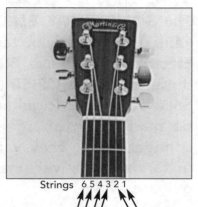

Strings 6 5 4 3 2 1

Bronze Wound onto Steel Strings   Plain Unwound Steel Strings

Once again, a reputable music store will be able to assist with providing you with the correct strings for your steel string guitar.

FITTING STEEL STRINGS

Fixing the string to the bridge: All steel strings have a steel ball tied to the end of the string. The ball is poked into a hole in the bridge and held into place with a bridge pin. The bridge pin has a slot cut into it to accommodate the string. Study the following diagrams.

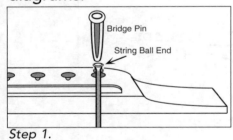

Bridge Pin

String Ball End

Step 1.

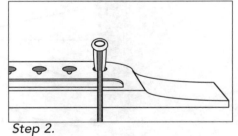

Step 2.

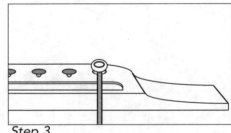

Step 3.

Tying the string to the tuning key:
When fitting a string to the tuning key the string is inserted through the tuning key hole only once.

The string is then neatly coiled 4 - 5 times around the barrel of the tuning key from the top of the barrel near the hole to the base of the barrel. *See below.*

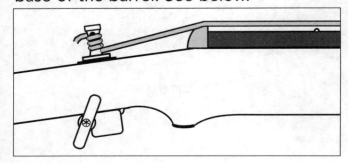

It is essential that the strings are wound onto the barrel of the tuning key from the correct side.

Turn the tuning key so the string is wound inward towards the the centre of the head not towards the outside of the head. Study the diagram.

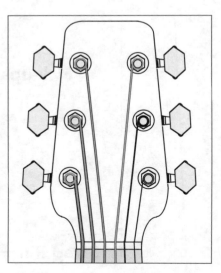

THE SOLID BODY ELECTRIC GUITAR

The **SOLID BODY ELECTRIC** is commonly used in Metal, Rock, Blues and Pop Music. Famous solid body guitars are the **GIBSON LES PAUL** and the **FENDER STRATOCASTER**. Electric guitars have **PICK-UPS** (a type of inbuilt microphone) and need to be played through an **AMPLIFIER** (amp) to be heard.

Solid body electric guitars are available in a variety of shapes, sizes and colours. They can be made from a large range of different timbers and use many string and pick-up configurations. They vary significantly in cost but most beginning solid body electric guitars are relatively inexpensive and are quite suitable for the early stages of electric guitar playing.

PARTS OF THE SOLID BODY GUITAR

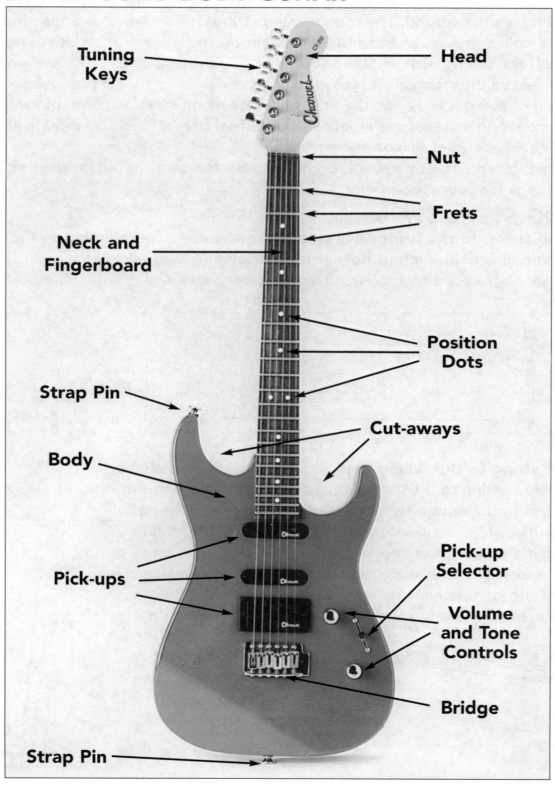

SOLID BODY ELECTRIC GUITAR SETUP

Solid Body Electric Guitar Strings

Generally solid body electric guitars are fitted with three unwound plain steel strings (strings 1- 3) and three nickel wound onto steel strings (strings 4 - 6). In almost all cases roundwound strings are used and are often a lighter gauge than steel guitar strings. This is to help with the need of bending the strings, a common technique with electric guitar playing.

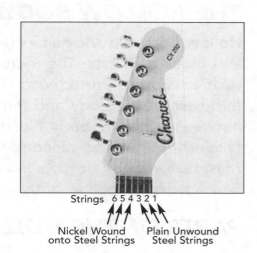

Strings 6 5 4 3 2 1

Nickel Wound onto Steel Strings — Plain Unwound Steel Strings

Fitting Solid Body Electric Strings

Fixing the string to the bridge: There are several variations on fixing an electric string to the bridge. Some electric guitar manufacturers use a bridge system specifically unique to their guitars. Some strings are inserted through holes at the back of the body, some are inserted through holes in a bridge tailpiece. With some more complex bridges such as the *Floyd Rose* bridge, the ball end is cut off and the string clamped to part of the bridge.

The most common bridge set-ups are shown. If your bridge is dissimilar to one of these types consult a qualified guitar repairer or an experienced guitarist.

Inserting string through hole at back of guitar body.

Fender Stratocaster style bridge.

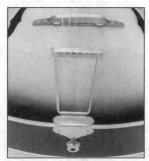

Bridge tailpiece style.

Floyd Rose Tremolo Bridge.

Tying the string to the tuning key:

Most electric guitar strings are fitted to the tuning key in exactly the same way a steel string acoustic string is fitted (see page 7). The string must also be neatly coiled 4 - 5 times around the barrel of the tuning key from the top of the barrel near the hole to the base of the barrel. Once again, it is important to take into consideration which side of the barrel the string is wound from. On electric guitar heads which have three tuning keys on each side, the strings are wound in the same way as a steel string guitar (see page 7). On electric guitars that have six tuning keys on the same side of the head, as with the Fender Stratocaster style, all the strings must be wound from the right side of the barrel (see adjacent diagram).

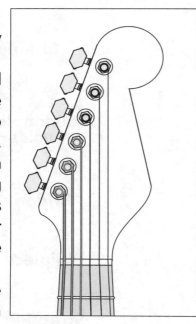

If the strings are wound correctly the string will tighten when the tuning key is turned in an anti-clockwise direction and loosen when the tuning key is turned in a clockwise direction.

10

THE HOLLOW BODY ELECTRIC GUITAR

Hollow body electric guitars (also known as semi-acoustic guitars) are mainly used by Jazz and Blues guitarists. The more popular hollow bodies are made by guitar manufacturers such as Gibson, Gretsch and Rickenbacker. They differ in various ways, such as shape, the thickness of the body and the amount of cut-aways in the body. A noticeable difference between a hollow body electric and a solid body electric is the use of a fixed bridge tailpiece, sometimes joined to the bottom of the guitar body, as part of the strap pin. Most hollow body electrics have soundholes in the same way a classical or steel string guitar has. A common hollow body soundhole style is the **f-hole** as shown in the photo below.

PARTS OF THE HOLLOW BODY GUITAR

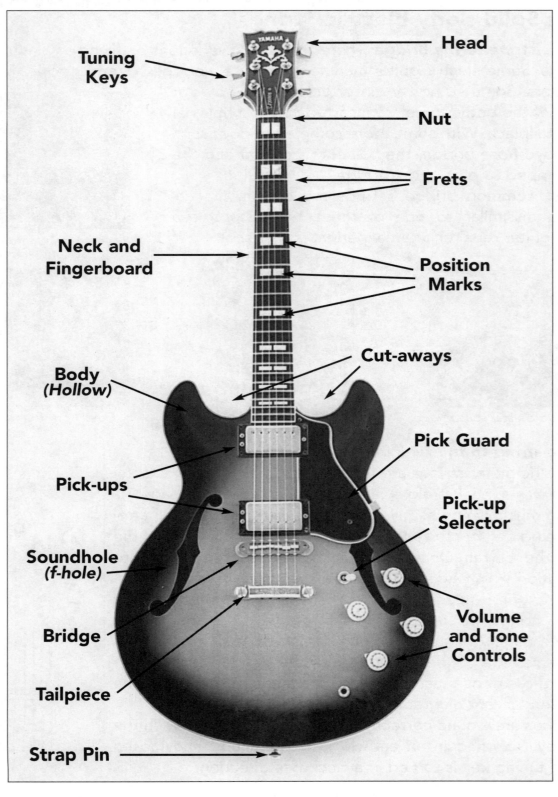

HOLLOW BODY ELECTRIC GUITAR SETUP

HOLLOW BODY ELECTRIC GUITAR STRINGS

Most hollow body electric guitars are fitted with three unwound plain steel strings (strings 1- 3) and three nickel wound onto steel strings (strings 4 - 6). Some Jazz guitarists however prefer the option of using a wound third string, as shown in the adjacent photo. This configuration, particularly used in conjunction with flatwound strings will give a more mellow sound.

Generally Jazz guitarists (and in many cases Blues players) will also opt for a heavier gauge string than that is used on solid body electric guitars.

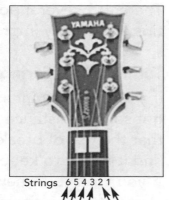

Strings 6 5 4 3 2 1

Nickel Wound onto Steel Strings   Plain Unwound Steel Strings

Fitting Hollow Body Electric Strings

Fixing the string to the bridge: The most common bridge setup on a hollow body electric is a fixed tailpiece system. The string is either inserted through a hole in the tailpiece and restrained by the ball end of the string or the ball end is secured in a slot cut out of the tail piece. Both tailpiece types make fitting the string simple.

Fixing the string to the tuning key: Strings are fixed to the tuning keys of a hollow body electric in the same way as a solid body electric (see page 9).

Fitting a string to a tailpiece.

GENERAL SETUP TIPS FOR ALL TYPES OF GUITARS

Other points to consider with the correct setting up of a guitar are outlined below.

TUNING KEYS

It is essential the tuning keys of the guitar are in good condition. The tuning keys should be lightly lubricated and any screws that are part of the mechanism correctly tightened.

THE NUT

The grooves that are cut out in the nut must be the correct size, shape and angle to help the string move freely through the groove when tightening and loosening the string.

THE BRIDGE SADDLE

The point at which the string makes contact with the saddle must also be smooth so the string can move freely when being adjusted.

STRING HEIGHT

The height of the strings from the fretboard (sometimes called the 'action') is very important to the feel of the guitar. If the strings are set too high, it will be more difficult to push the strings onto the fretboard. If the strings are set too low, the strings will rattle against the fretboard causing a buzzing noise. The height of the strings is determined by two things, the nut and the bridge saddle.

All the above adjustments should be carried out by a qualified guitar repairer. If your guitar is setup correctly it will be easier to tune and maintain its tune for longer.

BEFORE YOU BEGIN TO TUNE THE GUITAR

There are several points to consider before you begin tuning your guitar. The following tips will greatly improve your chances of successfully tuning your guitar.

Tuning New Strings

If you are a beginner and have fitted new strings to your guitar, it is recommended you get some assistance at first from an experienced guitar player. It is at this stage of tuning that the risk of breaking a string is highest. Once the strings are fitted and tuned you will find it easier to keep the guitar in tune by using minor adjustments.

If you wish to fit new strings to your guitar, try fitting one string at a time and tune the string after it is fitted. It is easier to tune one string to another string that is already at the correct pitch.

'Working In' New Strings

New strings will need to be 'worked in' after each fitting. This is specially helpful if you are fitting one new string at a time and you would like the string to stay in tune before fitting the next string.

Strings should be stretched by pulling them away from the fretboard a little. The string can also be stretched in sections along the string by stretching the string between the thumb and fingers of your right hand. Obviously do not over stretch the string as you could break the string. Ask an experienced guitarist for a lesson in this technique.

Once a string is fitted it should also be played a little to help with the settling down of the string. Sometimes it can take a few days for a new string to settle in but once it has, it should maintain its tune and only require minor adjustments.

Room Acoustics and Temperature

The sound of the room will assist with tuning. Try to tune the guitar in a quiet room so you can clearly hear the pitch and tone of each note as you are tuning. A useful tip is to practice tuning in the bathroom which often has the best acoustics in the house, helping to produce a strong, clear note.

Try to keep your guitar at a constant temperature. Moving your instrument from a cold room to a warmer room, or visa versa, can effect the pitch of the strings.

Slowly at First!

At the early stages of learning how to tune the guitar it is vital to approach it slowly and very carefully. A common error is to turn the wrong tuning key, causing another string that perhaps has already been tuned to be put out of tune. It also creates the risk of breaking a string. Before you adjust a tuning key, double check that you will in fact be turning the correct tuning key.

If your guitar has already been tuned, perhaps by your teacher or a friend, you should only need to make minor adjustments to the tuning key. Therefore it should not be necessary to turn the tuning key very much at all. If you find yourself turning a tuning key a lot, pause and rethink what you are doing. Chances are you could be doing something incorrectly.

Patience

Everyone has trouble with tuning a guitar in the beginning. Be patient and eventually you will be tuning your guitar, quickly, easily and accurately.

NOTES OF THE OPEN STRINGS

Before tuning your guitar it will be helpful to understand the names of the notes of the open strings. The diagrams below highlight the notes of the open strings for standard guitar tuning on a six and twelve string guitar. Each note is also shown as it appears on a music staff. Guitar music is covered in more detail later in the book.

STANDARD TUNING - 6 STRING GUITAR

The open strings of a 6 string guitar are tuned as shown.

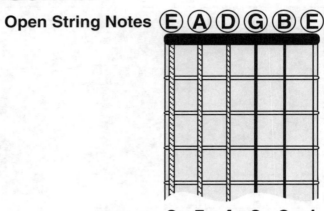

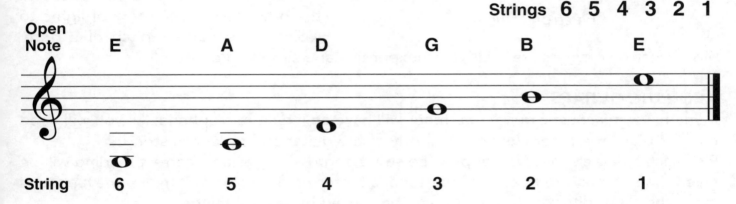

STANDARD TUNING - 12 STRING GUITAR

The open strings of a 12 string guitar are tuned as shown.

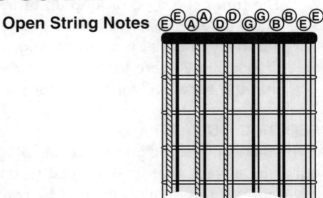

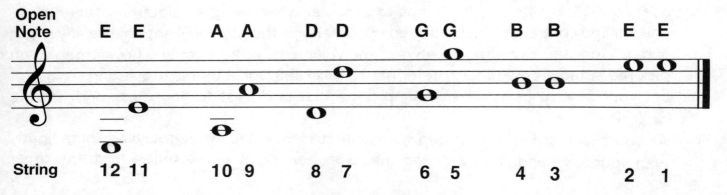

TUNING METHODS

There are many different methods to use to tune the guitar with some methods being more accurate than others. Some methods are relatively simple to use but some methods can be quite difficult and require a great deal of practice. The most popular methods of tuning the guitar will be covered in detail throughout the following pages.

USING AN ELECTRONIC TUNER

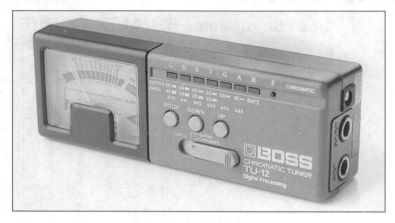

Electronic Tuner

The easiest and most accurate way to tune your guitar is by using an **electronic tuner**. An electronic tuner allows you to tune each string individually to the tuner, by indicating whether the notes are sharp (too high) or flat (too low). There are basically two types of electronic tuners. One type uses the position of a needle to indicate the correct pitch of a note and the other type uses a row of lights to indicate the correct pitch of a note.

Most electronic tuners are relatively inexpensive and simple to operate.

ACOUSTIC GUITARS

If you have an acoustic guitar, the tuner will have an inbuilt microphone. All you will need to do is place the tuner close to the body of the guitar and pick each string.

Pick each string cleanly. Do not pick the string aggressively as an incorrect reading will be given. Sometimes the needle of the tuner's meter or the lights will move unevenly and make the tuner difficult to use. This can be caused by several things;

1. The inbuilt microphone is not picking up the sound of the string enough. Experiment with the distance between the tuner and the body of the guitar.
2. The tuner could be picking up other sounds in the room. Ensure the room is quiet.
3. Make sure the battery is fully powered. It is easy to forget to turn off a tuner and as a battery gets flat a poor reading will be given.
4. Check that you are tuning the correct note, sometimes a string can be so out of tune that the tuner will mistake it for the wrong string.

ELECTRIC GUITARS

If you have an electric guitar you can plug it directly into the tuner. The tuner has a normal guitar input jack that enables you to connect your guitar lead. Most guitar tuners also have an extra hole allowing you to connect your tuner inline between your guitar and amplifier. Ensure that your guitar is plugged into the input jack and not the output jack that goes to the amplifier. Other things to consider when using an electronic tuner are:

1. The volume control should be turned up, otherwise the tuner will not receive any signal and not register. Experiment between the volume of your guitar and how strongly you pick the string. Some tuners prefer not to receive a signal that is too strong.
2. Set your pick-up switch. Use your pick-up that is closest to your neck and not the bridge.
3. As you pick a string, try to stop the other strings sounding by touching them lightly with your left hand. This will stop the tuner hearing any 'overtones' from the other strings.

TUNING YOUR GUITAR TO ANOTHER GUITAR

If you have available to you another guitar that is in tune you will be able to tune your guitar to it. Position yourself close to the other guitar in a quiet location.

1. Have someone pick the sixth string of the other guitar.
2. Listen carefully to the string, and try to focus on to the sound and pitch of the note.
3. While still focusing on that note, play the sixth string of your guitar and try to determine whether the sixth string on your guitar is higher in pitch or lower in pitch than the other string.
4. If you think the note is too low you will need to tighten your sixth string by turning its tuning key in an anti-clockwise direction. If you think the note is too high you will need to loosen your sixth string by turning its tuning key in a clockwise direction.
5. Double check that you are about to turn the correct tuning key. Play the sixth string again and turn the tuning key. Listen for the sound of the string rising or lowering in pitch.
6. When you are satisfied the notes are both the same continue with the other strings until all six strings have been tuned.

TUNING TIPS:

* You may find it easier to start with the first string rather than the sixth string.
* It is a good idea to always tune up to a note rather than down to a note. If you think the note is too high and needs to be lowered, detune the string so it is lower than the desired pitch then tune up to that note. In most cases you will find this easier and more accurate. Tuning up to the note also puts pressure on the tuning key keeping the string in tune longer.
* The above method is perfect for practising tuning if the other person is a competent tuner. They will be able to supervise you and check your tuning afterwards.

TUNING YOUR GUITAR TO THE CD

The first tracks on the accompanying CD contain recordings of the open strings of a guitar. On each track a string is played several times, giving you sufficient time to tune the corresponding string on your guitar to the sound of the note on the recording. You will also be able to program your CD player to repeat the specific track several times, increasing the amounts of times the note can be heard. The recording contains open string tuning notes for the three main types of guitar, the nylon string, steel string and electric. Beginners may find it easier to tune the strings of their guitar to the corresponding type of guitar on the recording. Each type of guitar has it own particular tonal characteristics and first time tuners will be able to hear the sound of a string that best matches their instrument. Also included on the recording are twelve tracks that correspond to the open twelve strings of a twelve string guitar. As with all tuning methods make sure you practice tuning to the CD in a quiet environment and double check that you are adjusting the correct tuning key before turning.

CD TRACKS 1 - 6:   NYLON STRING GUITAR

1 6th String **E Note** (Thickest string)

2 5th String **A Note**

3 4th String **D Note**

4 3rd String **G Note**

5 2nd String **B Note**

6 1st String **E Note** (Thinnest string)

TUNING YOUR GUITAR TO THE CD (CONT)

CD TRACKS 7 - 12: STEEL STRING GUITAR

7 6th String E Note

8 5th String A Note

9 4th String D Note

10 3rd String G Note

11 2nd String B Note

12 1st String E Note

CD TRACKS 13 - 18: ELECTRIC GUITAR

13 6th String E Note

14 5th String A Note

15 4th String D Note

16 3rd String G Note

17 2nd String B Note

18 1st String E Note

CD TRACKS 19 - 30: 12 STRING ACOUSTIC GUITAR

19 12th String E Note

20 11th String E Note

21 10th String A Note

22 9th String A Note

23 8th String D Note

24 7th String D Note

25 6th String G Note

26 5th String G Note

27 4th String B Note

28 3rd String B Note

29 2nd String E Note

30 1st String E Note

CHECKING YOUR TUNING WITH A CHORD

Once you are confident you have tuned all your strings it is a good idea to check your tuning by strumming a chord. Hold an open E Major chord as shown in the accompanying diagram and slowly strum across the strings. Listen to the sound of the E chord on the recording and compare it to the sound of your E chord.

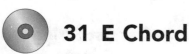

31 E Chord

TUNING YOUR GUITAR TO A PIANO OR KEYBOARD

Sometimes you may need to play along with another instrument. If you are playing along with another instrument, it is essential that your guitar be in tune with that instrument. Tune the open strings of your guitar to the corresponding notes of the accompanying instrument. E.g. to tune to a piano, tune the open 6th string to the E note on the piano, as shown on the keyboard diagram. Then either tune your guitar to itself from this note using the methods outlined on the following pages, or tune each string of your guitar to those notes of the piano shown on the keyboard diagram.

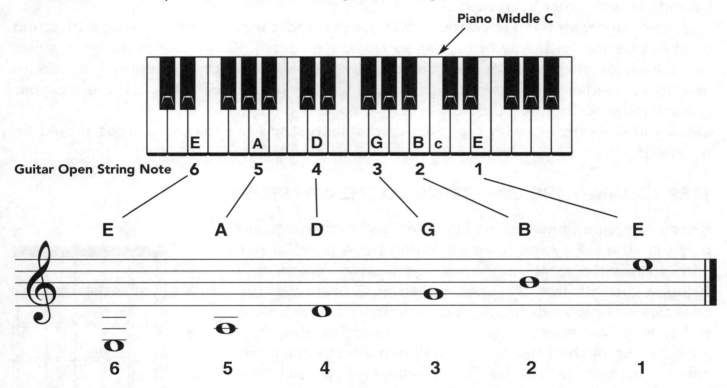

It is important to understand that guitar music is written one octave above piano music so the note range of the guitar can fit onto the treble clef. The open sixth string is notated below the third leger line underneath the music staff. If you play this note on the piano, as written on piano music it will be the E note immediately below the middle C note in the middle of the piano keyboard. This note will sound one octave higher than the open sixth string. Therefore if you wish to play a note on the piano that corresponds with a note on the guitar you must play the note one octave lower than written on the piano music.

On the accompanying CD a keyboard is used to play each of the notes that correspond to the open strings of your guitar. Each note of the keyboard will sustain for a considerable length of time giving you plenty of time to tune the string to the same pitch as the keyboard note.

CD TRACKS 32 - 37: ELECTRONIC KEYBOARD

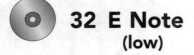 **32 E Note** (low)

 **33 A Note**

 **34 D Note**

 **35 G Note**

36 B Note

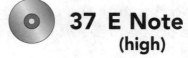 **37 E Note** (high)

TUNING THE GUITAR TO ITSELF

The methods outlined on the previous pages involved comparing each individual string to another note. However it is essential that you are able to tune the guitar to itself, meaning it is important to be able to check each string with the other strings on the guitar.

The following method requires the sixth string to be already in tune. If it is not possible to have the sixth string in tune using one of the previous methods discussed then it may be necessary to seek assistance with getting the sixth string as close as possible to concert pitch. It is acceptable to tune the guitar to itself, though not be at concert pitch, i.e. in tune with other instruments.

The most important thing to consider with this method is that the pitch of your sixth string must not be too far below or too far above concert pitch. Remember that if your guitar has already been correctly tuned and you have followed correct maintenance procedure as outlined earlier then your strings should only require minor tuning. Therefore your guitar should not be too far below or above concert pitch.

Once you are satisfied with the pitch of the sixth string the following steps should be followed;

STEP 1 TUNING THE 5TH STRING TO THE 6TH STRING

Place a left hand finger on the 6th string at the fifth fret, and play the string. Play the open 5th string (an A note). If this note sounds the same as the note you played on the 6th string at the fifth fret, the open 5th string is in tune. If the open 5th string sounds higher, it means that it is sharp. Turn the tuning key slowly in a clockwise direction therefore lowering the pitch of the note. If the open 5th string sounds lower, it means that it is flat. Turn the tuning key slowly in a counter-clockwise direction thus raising the pitch of the note. Note: Ensure that you are turning the correct tuning key and listen to the string change pitch as you turn the tuning key. Play the two strings again and compare the notes. Keep doing this until the open A string sounds the same as the A note at the fifth fret of the 6th string.

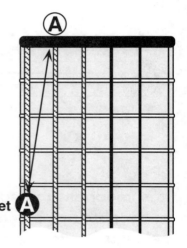

5th Fret

STEP 2 TUNING THE 4TH STRING TO THE 5TH STRING

Place a left hand finger on the 5th string at the fifth fret, and play the string. Play the open 4th string (a D note). If this note sounds the same as the note you played on the 5th string at the fifth fret, the open 4th string is in tune. If the open 4th string sounds higher, it means that it is sharp. Turn the tuning key slowly in a clockwise direction therefore lowering the pitch of the note. If the open 4th string sounds lower, it means that it is flat. Turn the tuning key slowly in a counter-clockwise direction thus raising the pitch of the note. Play the two strings again and compare the notes. Keep doing this until the open D string sounds the same as the D note at the fifth fret of the 5th string.

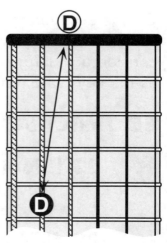

5th Fret

STEP 3 TUNING THE 3RD STRING TO THE 4TH STRING

Now place a left hand finger on the 4th string at the fifth fret, and play the string. Play the open 3rd string (a G note). If this note sounds the same as the note you played on the 4th string at the fifth fret, the open 3rd string is in tune. If the open 3rd string sounds higher, turn the tuning key slowly in a clockwise direction to lower the pitch of the note. If the open 3rd string sounds lower, turn the tuning key slowly in a counter-clockwise direction to raise the pitch of the note. Play the two strings again and compare the notes. Keep doing this until the open G string sounds the same as the G note at the fifth fret of the 4th string.

5th Fret

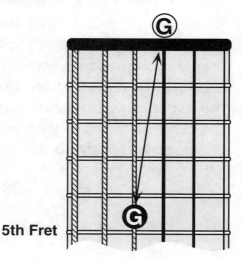

STEP 4 TUNING THE 2ND STRING TO THE 3RD STRING

Now place a left hand finger on the 3rd string at the fourth fret, and play the string. Play the open 2nd string (a B note). If this note sounds the same as the note you played on the 3rd string at the fourth fret, the open 2nd string is in tune. If the open 2nd string sounds higher, turn the tuning key slowly in a clockwise direction to lower the pitch of the note. If the open 2nd string sounds lower, turn the tuning key slowly in a counter-clockwise direction to raise the pitch of the note. Play the two strings again and compare the notes. Keep doing this until the open B string sounds the same as the B note at the fourth fret of the 3rd string.

4th Fret

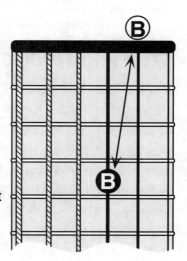

STEP 5 TUNING THE 1ST STRING TO THE 2ND STRING

Finally, place a left hand finger on the 2nd string at the fifth fret, and play the string. Play the open 1st string (an E note). If this note sounds the same as the note you played on the 2nd string at the fifth fret, the open 1st string is in tune. If the open 1st string sounds higher, turn the tuning key slowly in a clockwise direction to lower the pitch of the note. If the open 1st string sounds lower, turn the tuning key slowly in a counter-clockwise direction to raise the pitch of the note. Play the two strings again and compare the notes. Keep doing this until the open E string sounds the same as the E note at the fifth fret of the 2nd string.

5th Fret

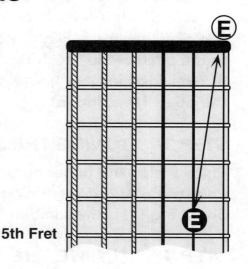

TUNING THE GUITAR TO A TUNING FORK

Tuning your guitar to a tuning fork is one of the least expensive methods of ensuring your guitar will be at concert pitch. A tuning fork is a small metal object in the shape of a fork that is hit against something solid and placed on the bridge or soundboard of the guitar producing a note that the first string can be tuned to. The other strings are then tuned to the 1st string. The most common tuning fork is an A tuning fork that gives the note A on the 5th fret of the first string. An E tuning fork is also available which produces the note of the open 1st string (E).

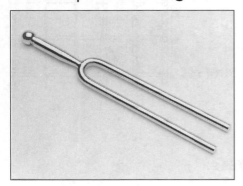
Tuning Fork

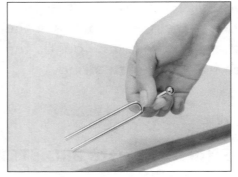
Strike Tuning Fork

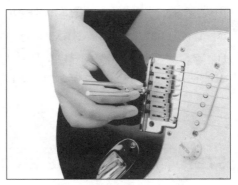
Place Tuning Fork on Guitar

STEP 1   TUNING THE 1ST STRING TO THE TUNING FORK

Play either the open 1st string (E), or the fifth fret of the 1st string (A) depending on which tuning fork you have. Immediately after picking the string strike the tuning fork against something solid and place the fork on the bridge of the guitar. Compare the pitch of the string and the sound produced by the tuning fork. If the pitch of the tuning fork sounds the same as the note you played on the 1st string the string is in tune. If the 1st string sounds higher, it means that it is sharp. Turn the tuning key slowly in a clockwise direction therefore lowering the pitch of the note. If the 1st string sounds lower, it means that it is flat. Turn the tuning key slowly in a counter-clockwise direction to raise the pitch of the note.

STEP 2   TUNING THE 2ND STRING TO THE 1ST STRING

The next step is to tune the rest of the strings to the 1st string. This is done in the same way as tuning the guitar to itself, as explained on the previous pages, except the strings are tuned in the reverse order. Place a left hand finger on the 2nd string at the fifth fret, and play the string. Play the open 1st string. This time you will need to tune the 2nd string to the pitch of the 1st string. Turn the tuning key for the 2nd string in the correct direction, as explained in step 1, until the note on the fifth fret of the 2nd string (E) is the same as the open 1st string (E).

STEP 3   TUNING THE 3RD STRING TO THE 2ND STRING

Place a left hand finger on the 3rd string at the 4th fret, and play the string. Play the open 2nd string. Adjust the tuning key for the 3rd string until the note on the fourth fret of the 3rd string (B) is the same as the open 2nd string (B).

STEP 4   TUNING THE 4TH STRING TO THE 3RD STRING

Place a left hand finger on the 4th string at the 5th fret, and play the string. Play the open 3rd string. Adjust the tuning key for the 4th string until the note on the fifth fret of the 4th string (G) is the same as the open 3rd string (G).

STEP 5   TUNING THE 5TH STRING TO THE 4TH STRING

Place a left hand finger on the 5th string at the 5th fret, and play the string. Play the open 4th string. Adjust the tuning key for the 5th string until the note on the fifth fret of the 5th string (D) is the same as the open 4th string (D).

STEP 6   TUNING THE 6TH STRING TO THE 5TH STRING

Finally place a left hand finger on the 6th string at the 5th fret, and play the string. Play the open 5th string. Adjust the tuning key for the 6th string until the note on the fifth fret of the 6th string (A) is the same as the open 5th string (A). This step and each of the previous steps can be shown in the adjacent diagram.

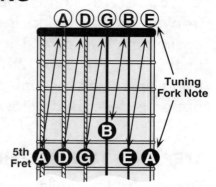

TUNING THE GUITAR TO PITCH PIPES

Pitch pipes produce notes that correspond to each of the six open strings. Tuning with pitch pipes is another inexpensive method of tuning the guitar to concert pitch. The sound of the pitch pipes however is quite different to the sound of the guitar strings so you may find it difficult at first to distinguish the difference between the two sounds.

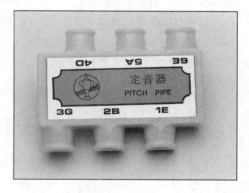

Pitch Pipes

TUNING VIBRATIONS

A useful tip when tuning the guitar is to listen for a vibrating or "wah wah" sound when two notes are ringing together. Each note vibrates at a different speed, or different amount of cycles per second. When two different notes are ringing together they vibrate at different speeds and cause a wah wah sound. This sound can be difficult to detect but if you play both notes loud enough, and you have complete quiet, you might be able to hear the sound, or even feel the sound as a pulse through the body of the guitar.

This vibration can be shown as a wave form. If the two notes played together are a long way out of tune with each other you will hear the wah wah sound vibrating quite fast.

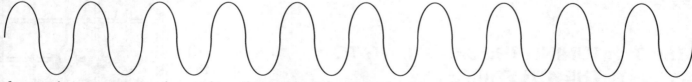

If you do manage to hear the vibrations listen to the speed as you adjust the tuning key. If you hear the vibration increase then you are getting further out of tune, i.e. you are turning the tuning key the wrong way. If the vibration gets slower, meaning the wah wah sounds become less frequent then the two notes are getting closer together. The wave form below represents two notes almost in tune with each other.

When both notes are in tune with each other the wah wah sound should virtually disappear.

TUNING WITH HARMONICS

Tuning with harmonics is popular tuning method with experienced guitarists. This option is difficult at first to execute but with practice will prove to be a useful and accurate tuning method. A harmonic is a 'bell like' sound that is produced by lightly touching the string directly above the fretwire as the string is picked. The string is not pressed against the fretboard. The most common harmonics are found at the 5th, 7th and 12th frets. There are many options for using harmonics for tuning with harmonics. The most common option is described below.

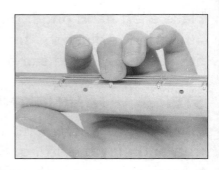

Touch string lightly above the fretwire.

STEP 1   TUNING THE 5TH STRING TO THE 6TH STRING

This method is similar to tuning the guitar to itself (page 18) as the strings are tuned in order from the sixth string to the first string. The 6th string will need to be in tune using methods outlined earlier in the book. Play the harmonic on the fifth fret of the 6th string. Now play the harmonic on the seventh fret of the 5th string. Adjust the tuning key for the 5th string until the harmonic on the fifth fret of the 6th string (E) is the same as the harmonic on the seventh fret of the 5th string (E).

 38   E Harmonic

STEP 2   TUNING THE 4TH STRING TO THE 5TH STRING

Play the harmonic on the fifth fret of the 5th string. Now play the harmonic on the seventh fret of the 4th string. Adjust the tuning key for the 4th string until the harmonic on the fifth fret of the 5th string (A) is the same as the harmonic on the seventh fret of the 4th string (A).

 39   A Harmonic

STEP 3   TUNING THE 3RD STRING TO THE 4TH STRING

Play the harmonic on the fifth fret of the 4th string. Now play the harmonic on the seventh fret of the 3rd string. Adjust the tuning key for the 3rd string until the harmonic on the fifth fret of the 4th string (D) is the same as the harmonic on the seventh fret of the 3rd string (D).

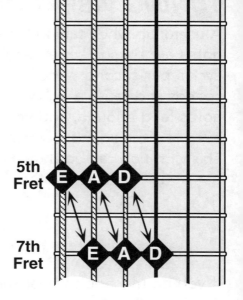

 40   D Harmonic

The final steps of this method involve comparing the seventh fret harmonic of the 6th string with the open 2nd string and the seventh fret harmonic of the 5th string with the open 1st string.

STEP 4   TUNING THE 2ND STRING TO THE 6TH STRING

Play the harmonic on the seventh fret of the 6th string. Now play the open 2nd string. Adjust the tuning key for the 2nd string until the harmonic on the seventh fret of the 6th string (B) is the same as the open 2nd string (B).

 41   B Harmonic

STEP 5   TUNING THE 1ST STRING TO
THE 5TH STRING

Play the harmonic on the seventh fret of the 5th string. Now play the open 1st string. Adjust the tuning key for the 1st string until the harmonic on the seventh fret of the 5th string (E) is the same as the open 1st string (E).

 42   E Harmonic

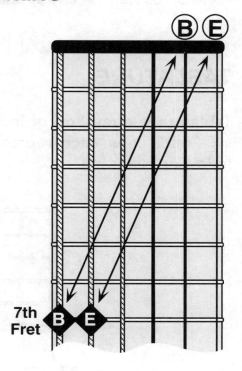

7th
Fret

HOW TO READ MUSIC

There are two methods used to write guitar music. First is the **TRADITIONAL MUSIC NOTATION** method (using music notes, ♩) and second is **TABLATURE.** Most guitarists find Tablature easier to read, however, it is very worthwhile to learn to read traditional music notation as well. Nearly all sheet music you buy in a store is written in traditional notation.

TABLATURE

Tablature is a method of indicating the position of notes on the fretboard. There are six "tab" lines each representing one of the six strings of the guitar. Study the following diagram.

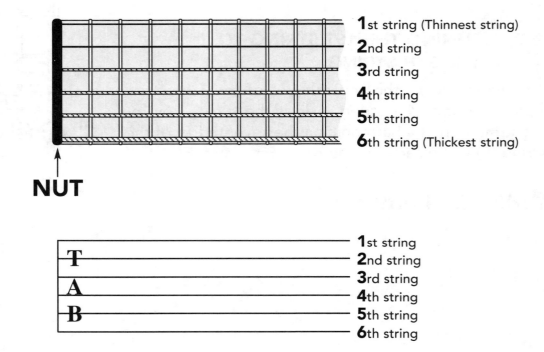

1st string (Thinnest string)
2nd string
3rd string
4th string
5th string
6th string (Thickest string)

NUT

T
A
B

1st string
2nd string
3rd string
4th string
5th string
6th string

When a number is placed on one of the lines, it indicates the fret location of a note e.g.

This indicates the open 3rd string (a G note).

This indicates the 3rd fret of the 5th string (a C note).

This indicates the 1st fret of the 1st string (an F note).

MUSIC NOTATION

These five lines are called the **STAFF** or the **STAVE**.

THE TREBLE CLEF

 This symbol is called a **treble clef**. There is a treble clef at the beginning of every line of guitar music.

MUSIC NOTES

There are only seven letters used for notes in music. They are:

A B C D E F G

These notes are known as the **musical alphabet.** Guitar music notes are written in the spaces and on the lines of the treble staff.

THE QUARTER NOTE

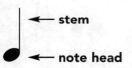

This music note is called a **quarter note**. A quarter note lasts for **one beat**.

THE TREBLE STAFF

A staff with a treble clef written on it is called a **treble staff**.

NOTE AND REST VALUES

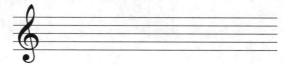

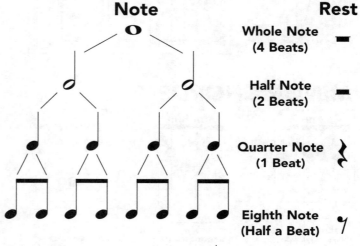

Note	Rest
Whole Note (4 Beats)	
Half Note (2 Beats)	
Quarter Note (1 Beat)	
Eighth Note (Half a Beat)	

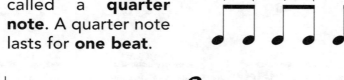

To remember the notes on the lines of the staff, say:
Every **G**ood **B**oy **D**eserves **F**ruit.

The notes in the spaces spell:
F A C E

BAR LINES are drawn across the staff, which divides the music into sections called **BARS** or **MEASURES**. A **DOUBLE BAR LINE** signifies either the end of the music, or the end of an important section of it.

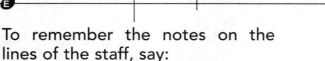

THE FOUR FOUR TIME SIGNATURE

 These two numbers are called the **four four time signature.** They are placed after the treble clef. The $\frac{4}{4}$ time signature tells you there are four beats in each bar. There are **four** quarter notes in one bar of music in $\frac{4}{4}$ time.

CHORD CHART

The following chord chart shows all the important basic chords. For a complete knowledge of chords and rhythm techniques see the following books (detailed on pages 28 and 29) **Progressive Guitar Chords, Progressive Rhythm Guitar, Progressive Guitar Method: Rhythm** and **Progressive Guitar Method: Chords.**

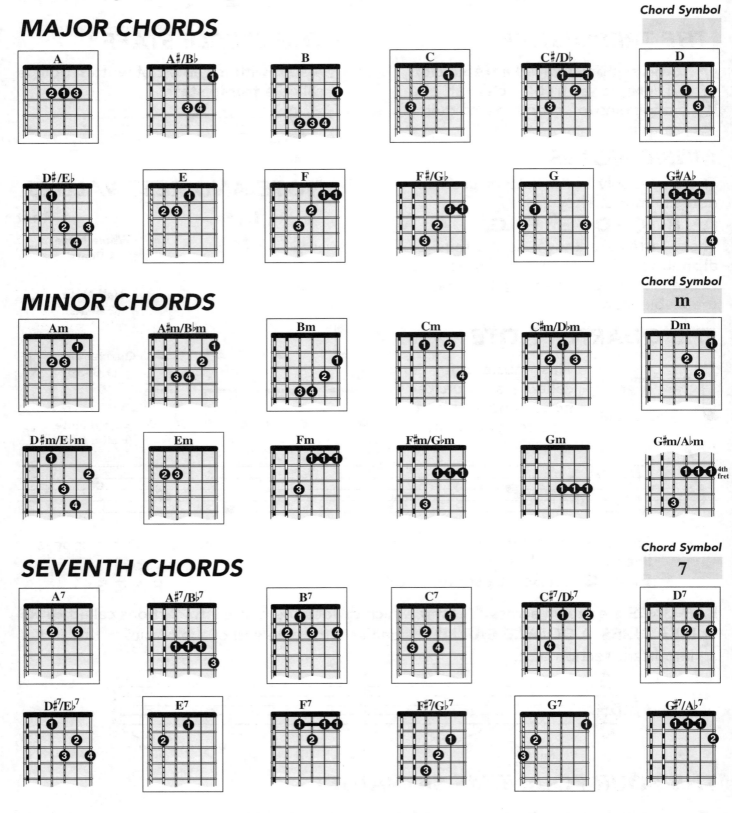

1 indicates 1st finger   **3** indicates 3rd finger   A broken line indicates that a
2 indicates 2nd finger   **4** indicates 4th finger   string is not to be played.

STYLES OF PLAYING GUITAR

The guitar is the most versatile musical instrument and can be used to play virtually all music styles including Classical, Rock, Pop, Blues, Jazz, Country, Funk, Metal, Folk, Rock 'n' Roll etc. There are many different styles of playing guitar and all these styles can be played on any type of guitar. You would usually play lead on an electric guitar but you could play lead on a classical guitar or you could play fingerpicking style on an electric guitar. It all depends upon the sound you are looking for.

There are many guitar books available in the **Progressive** series some of which are listed on the following pages. Available at all good music stores or available from our website at **www.learntoplaymusic.com**.

PREVIEWS: On the accompanying recording of this book you will be able to hear selected previews taken directly from the recording of each of the following books. Each preview will give you an insight into each of the many styles that can be played on the guitar.

NOTE READING

 43   Previews

PROGRESSIVE GUITAR METHOD BOOK 1

The Progressive Guitar Method is a series of books designed to take the Guitar student from a beginner level through to a professional standard of playing. All books are carefully graded, lesson by lesson methods which assume no prior knowledge on your behalf. Within the series all styles and techniques of guitar playing are covered, including reading music, playing chords and rhythms, lead guitar and fingerpicking.

Progressive Guitar Method Book 1 assumes you have no prior knowledge of music or playing the guitar. This book will teach you the notes on each of the six strings, together with basic elements of music theory including time signatures, note values, sharps, flats and the chromatic scale. This theory is essential to help you understand the guitar and can be applied to solve practical problems, hence speeding up your progress. This book also has special sections on tuning, how to read sheet music and a chord chart. Upon its completion you will have a solid understanding of guitar. All guitarists should know all of the information in this book. A tab version of this book is also available.

 44   Previews

PROGRESSIVE GUITAR METHOD: SUPPLEMENT

Progressive Guitar Method Book 1: Supplement is designed to be used in conjunction with Progressive Guitar Method Book 1 and contains an extra 70 songs to play, and 8 more lessons including information on major scales, keys, triplets, $\frac{6}{8}$ time, sixteenth notes, syncopation and swing rhythms. All guitarists should know all of the information in this book.

In conjunction with this book you can use other books in the progressive series to learn about tablature reading, lead guitar playing, fingerpicking, bar chords, slide and classical guitar styles as well as music theory and different styles such as Rock, Blues, Country, Jazz, Metal and Funk.

45   Previews

PROGRESSIVE GUITAR METHOD: THEORY

A comprehensive, introduction to music theory as it applies to the guitar. Covers reading traditional music, rhythm notation and tablature, along with learning the notes on the fretboard, how to construct chords and scales, transposition, musical terms and playing in all keys.

CHORDS

 46   Previews

PROGRESSIVE GUITAR CHORDS

Progressive Guitar Chords contains over 180 pages and is the ultimate reference manual for guitar chords. This book contains thousands of chord diagrams including open chords for beginners, bar chords for the semi-advanced player and moveable chords for the advanced player. Includes a wealth of information on music theory for guitarists providing a thorough knowledge of scales, keys, chord construction etc. Also includes a selection of chord progressions using many of the chords shown in the book.

47   Previews

PROGRESSIVE GUITAR METHOD: CHORDS

Progressive Guitar Method: Chords is a chord dictionary containing the most useful open, bar, and Jazz chord shapes of all the most commonly used chord types including major, minor, seventh, sixth, major seventh, minor seventh, suspended, ninth, etc. Also contains special sections on tuning, how to read sheet music and the use of a capo. It also includes an easy chord table, chord formula and chord symbol chart.

 48   Previews

PROGRESSIVE GUITAR METHOD: BAR CHORDS

Progressive Guitar Method: Bar Chords introduces the most popular and most useful bar chord shapes used by Rock/Pop/Country and Blues guitarists. All the important chord types are shown including major, minor, seventh, sixth, major seventh, minor seventh, suspended, ninth, etc. Root 6 and Root 5 bar chords are discussed in detail along with suggested rhythm patterns including percussive strums, damping and sixteenth note rhythms. Also covers Rock/Power chords, rhythm techniques and basic Jazz chord shapes.

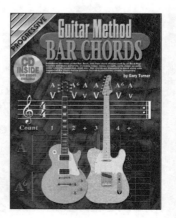

RHYTHM

 49 Previews

PROGRESSIVE RHYTHM GUITAR

Progressive Rhythm Guitar contains over 140 pages and is the complete instruction manual for Rhythm guitar. Covers Rock styles, Rhythm patterns and techniques, playing in a group, chord substitution, reading sheet music and theory as it relates to the Rhythm guitarist. Uses the most useful open, bar, and Jazz chord shapes of all the most commonly used chord types including major, minor, seventh, sixth, major seventh, minor seventh, suspended, ninth, etc.

 50 Previews

PROGRESSIVE GUITAR METHOD: RHYTHM

Progressive Guitar Method: Rhythm assumes you have no prior knowledge of music or playing the guitar. Starting with the different types of guitars available and the different styles of playing you are introduced to all the important open chord shapes for major, minor, seventh, sixth, major seventh, minor seventh, suspended, diminished and augmented chords. Learn to play over 50 chord progressions, including 12 Bar Blues and Turnaround progressions.

LEAD

 51 Previews

PROGRESSIVE LEAD GUITAR

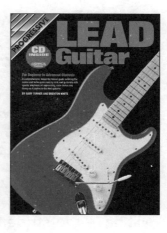

Progressive Lead Guitar will provide you with an essential guide into the scales and techniques used by Lead guitarists. Within the three sections of this book, a lesson by lesson structure has been used to give a clear and carefully graded method of study. Covers Major, Minor, Pentatonic scales and lead guitar techniques such as the hammer-on, pull-off, slide, bends, vibrato, pick tremolo etc. Features several great sounding solos incorporating the scales and techniques studied throughout the book.

 52 Previews

PROGRESSIVE GUITAR METHOD: LEAD

Progressive Guitar Method: Lead will show you the 12 bar Blues progression, using riffs and variations incorporating, quarter, eighth, sixteenth notes and triplets, along with ties, rests, shuffle and syncopated timing. Teaches scales and patterns over the entire fretboard so that you can improvise against major, minor and Blues progressions in any key. All the common lead guitar techniques are taught and includes special sections on jamming progressions, music notation, scales and notes on the entire fretboard.

53 Previews

PROGRESSIVE LEAD GUITAR LICKS

Progressive Lead Guitar Licks features over 110 lead guitar licks incorporating the styles and techniques used by the world's best lead guitar players. The licks are set out in order of difficulty to assist lead guitar players of all levels. The emphasis in this volume is to provide a vast variety of music styles to enable you to fit in with any music performing or recording situation.

The first four sections cover Rock, Blues, Heavy Metal and Country. At the end of each section is a lead guitar solo, showing how the licks and techniques throughout each section can be used to create a lead guitar solo.

 54 Previews

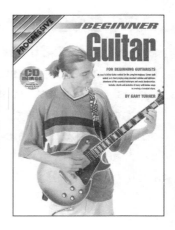

PROGRESSIVE BEGINNER GUITAR

An easy to follow Guitar method for the complete beginner. Covers both melody and chord playing using standard notation and tablature. Introduces all the essential techniques and music fundamentals. Includes chords and melodies of many well known songs in a variety of musical styles.

 55 Previews

PROGRESSIVE ELECTRIC GUITAR

An innovative approach to learning the electric guitar which incorporates the volume and tone controls, the pickup selector switch, effects and amplifier settings into learning music from the very beginning. Explains and demonstrates all the essential chords, scales, rhythms and expressive techniques such as slides, bends, trills and vibrato. Also contains lessons on understanding the bass and drums and how to create parts which work with them. This book will have the student ready to play in a band in next to no time.

 56 Previews

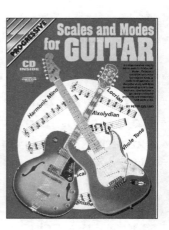

PROGRESSIVE SCALES AND MODES

A complete system for learning any scale, mode or chord and makes it easy to memorise any new new sound as well as building a solid visual and aural foundation of both the theory and the guitar fretboard. Shows you how to use each scale as well as how and why it fits with a particular chord or progression. Also contains jam along progressions for every scale and mode presented in the book.

ROCK

 57 Previews

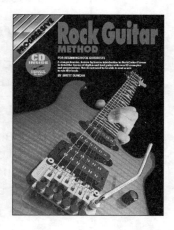

PROGRESSIVE ROCK GUITAR METHOD

Progressive Rock Guitar Method will introduce you to the exciting world of Rock guitar. It will not be necessary to have any previous knowledge of the guitar, as this book is suitable for the beginner. This book deals with the two main classifications of Rock guitar, rhythm and lead. You will become familiar with both subjects as you work your way through the book.

Rhythm guitar, being the technique of strumming chords, is explained clearly and simply throughout the book, with the help of an *Easy Read* system involving arrows.

 58 Previews

PROGRESSIVE ROCK GUITAR LICKS

Progressive Rock Guitar Licks incorporates the many different techniques, scales and patterns used in modern styles of Rock guitar. There are five sections throughout the book, each dealing with one of the five popular Rock lead guitar patterns. The licks in each section are examples of how each pattern can be applied to each pattern. At the end of each section is a Rock guitar solo, which fully shows how the licks and techniques learnt throughout each section can be used to create a Rock guitar solo.

 59 Previews

PROGRESSIVE ROCK GUITAR TECHNIQUE

This book continues on from *Progressive Rock Guitar Method*, dealing with all the Rhythm and Lead guitar styles of Rock. Rhythm guitar will be developed further by learning Bar chords, Rock progressions and advanced rhythm techniques. Lead guitarists will learn scale patterns, licks and solos using techniques such as Hammer-ons, Pull-offs, Slides, Bends, Vibrato and Double Note Licks. All licks and solos are clearly notated using standard music notation and 'Easy Read' guitar tab.

BLUES

 60 Previews

PROGRESSIVE BLUES LEAD GUITAR METHOD

Progressive Blues Lead Guitar Method takes a unique approach to learning Blues lead guitar. The most common scale used in Blues – the minor pentatonic scale, is used immediately to create great sounding Blues licks and solos. The minor pentatonic scale is learned in five basic positions which cover the whole fretboard, along with a variety of licks and solos demonstrating all the important techniques such as slides, vibrato and note bending, as used by all the great Blues players.

61 Previews

PROGRESSIVE BLUES GUITAR

A great introduction to the world of Blues Guitar. Covers all the essential rhythms used in Blues and R&B along with turnarounds, intros and endings, and gaining control of 12 and 8 bar Blues forms. Also explains and demonstrates the Blues scale, major and minor pentatonic scales and 7th arpeggios in a logical system for playing over the entire fretboard. Contains all the classic Blues sounds such as note bending, slides, and vibrato demonstrated in over 100 licks and solos in a variety of Blues styles.

 62 Previews

PROGRESSIVE BLUES GUITAR LICKS

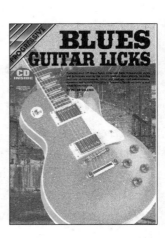

Packed full of Blues guitar licks and solos incorporating styles and techniques used by the world's greatest Blues players. Includes sections on turnarounds, intro's and endings, call and response, dynamics and learning from other instruments. The licks cover a variety of styles such as shuffles, traditional slow Blues, Boogie, Jazz style Blues and R&B and Funk grooves. Also includes examples demonstrating how different licks can be put together to form whole solos, opening up endless possibilities for improvisation.

 63 Previews

PROGRESSIVE BLUES LEAD GUITAR TECHNIQUE

A comprehensive introduction to all the sounds used in Blues lead guitar playing. Demonstrates all essential scales and arpeggios in a system which covers the whole fretboard and enables you to easily understand what you are playing. You will also learn all the important rhythms used by Blues players and systems for analyzing both rhythms and scale degrees. The book includes several solos demonstrating how the licks and techniques in each section can be used to create whole solos. Also includes several Jam along progressions.

 64 Previews

PROGRESSIVE BLUES GUITAR SOLOS

Features a wide variety of Licks and Solos incorporating styles and techniques used by the world's greatest Blues players. Licks are set out in a progressive manner to assist Blues guitar players of all levels. The book includes sections on turnarounds, intro's and endings, playing over stops, call and response, and the use of dynamics. Covers all the important scales and arpeggios used in Blues. Styles include shuffles, traditional slow Blues, Jazz style Blues, along with R & B and Funk grooves. Many of the licks and solos are written in the styles of Blues legends like BB King, Albert Collins, Otis Rush, and Stevie Ray Vaughan.

65 Previews

PROGRESSIVE BLUES RHYTHM GUITAR METHOD

A comprehensive introduction to the world of Blues rhythm guitar playing. Uses a variety of left and right hand techniques to help the student gain control of timing and rhythms which are essential to creating good Blues rhythm parts. The book contains a study of both open and moveable chord shapes, before moving on to single and double note riffs which include many of the classic Blues sounds.

 66 Previews

PROGRESSIVE BLUES RHYTHM TECHNIQUE

Features great rhythm parts in a wide variety of Blues and R&B styles including shuffles, boogie, jump Blues, traditional slow Blues, Rock and Roll, Jazz and Funk. Shows you how to create rhythm parts using both chords and single note riffs and how to fit your parts to the style and instrumental combination you are playing with. Anyone who completes this book will be well on the way to being a great rhythm player.

HEAVY METAL

 67 Previews

PROGRESSIVE HEAVY METAL TECHNIQUES

A comprehensive, easy to follow guide, introducing all the important techniques used the world's best HEAVY METAL guitarists. Including: Bends, vibrato, two handed tapping, slurs, trills, speed picking, harmonics, dampening and used of the temolo arm. You do not need to read music notes to read this book.

 68 Previews

PROGRESSIVE HEAVY METAL LICKS

Featuring over 100 'classic' Heavy Metal guitar licks and tricks played in the styles of the world's best Heavy Metal guitarists. These licks are particularly useful as reinforcements of tehnical aspects of playing Heavy Metal guitar, a source of ideas for your own licks and solos, practical excersices and a source of teaching material.
Includes tablature reading as well as standard music notation.

34

COUNTRY

 69 Previews

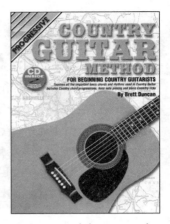

PROGRESSIVE COUNTRY GUITAR METHOD

Progressive Country Guitar Method covers all the basic essentials of Country guitar. It will not be necessary to have any previous knowledge of the guitar, as this book is suitable for the complete beginner. Experienced guitarists however, who perhaps have not tackled this style before, will find this manual invaluable as an introduction to the basics of Country guitar. From this book you will learn how to play basic chords, country progressions and rhythms, bass note picking, basic Country lead guitar licks and techniques. Upon its completion you will have a solid understanding of Country guitar and be ready to further your study of this style.

 70 Previews

PROGRESSIVE COUNTRY GUITAR TECHNIQUE

Progressive Country Guitar Technique is a continuation from *Progressive Country Guitar Method*. This book will cover more advanced chords, rhythms and lead techniques used in Country guitar. For rhythm guitar playing the most common Bar chords and rhythms are introduced throughout the book. For Country lead guitar players the most common lead guitar patterns are introduced and several interesting Country lead guitar solos are featured. The final lesson covers Fingerpicking and Slide guitar.

FUNK

 71 Previews

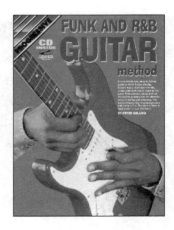

PROGRESSIVE FUNK R&B GUITAR METHOD

This book demonstrates many of the classic Funk sounds, using both rhythm and lead playing, since a good Funk player needs to be equally comfortable with both. A variety of chord forms are introduced within a framework that quickly allows the student to play confidently over the entire fretboard. Features an innovative approach to learning rhythms and applying them to riffs and grooves.

 72 Previews

PROGRESSIVE FUNK R&B GUITAR TECHNIQUE

Covers a range of exciting chord sounds essential to Funk, along with the Dorian and Mixolydian modes and the use of harmonic intervals such as 6ths, 3rds, 4ths, octaves and tritones. Also features a thorough study of rhythms and right hand techniques such as percussive strumming and string muting. A range of Funk styles are examined, as well as some great Soul and R&B sounds.

JAZZ

73 Previews

PROGRESSIVE JAZZ GUITAR

Progressive Jazz Guitar is a simple and logical introduction to Jazz chord playing for the beginning Jazz guitarist. Covers all important chord types including Major, Minor, all types of Seventh chord, Ninth, Eleventh, Thirteenth, and Altered chords. Each chord type is presented separately along with its formula and relationship to the major scale. Typical chord progressions are given with each new chord type, gradually building up a whole system for Jazz rhythm playing either solo or in a group situation.

FINGERPICKING

74 Previews

PROGRESSIVE FINGERPICKING GUITAR

Progressive Fingerpicking Guitar will provide you with an essential guide into the most common fingerpicking patterns used by modern folk and acoustic guitarists including alternating thumb and arpeggio styles. A lesson by lesson structure has been used to give a clear and carefully graded method of study. Features many interesting chord progressions and great sounding solos in a variety of styles. The fingerpicking patterns taught are universal in that they may be applied to other chord progressions involving bar or 'jazz' flavoured chords.

75 Previews

PROGRESSIVE GUITAR METHOD: FINGERPICKING

Progressive Guitar Method: Fingerpicking will introduce you to right hand fingerpicking patterns that can be applied to any chord, chord progression or song. Playing chord shapes with these patterns will allow you to provide accompaniment for any song. Covers fingerpicking in the styles of Folk, Country, Rock, Pop, Blues and Ragtime. Extra sections include Notes on the Guitar Fretboard, How to Read Music, How to Transpose and a Chord Chart.

76 Previews

PROGRESSIVE FINGERPICKING GUITAR LICKS

Progressive Fingerpicking Guitar Licks features over 50 Fingerpicking licks, riffs and solos which can be applied to Rock, Blues, Country, Folk styles etc. Incorporates licks based upon chord shapes and shows how the licks can be applied to popular chord progressions. Covers the most common fingerpicking styles including the alternating thumb style, monotonic bass style and includes several popular open tunings. Features both standard music notation and tablature.

SLIDE

 77 Previews

PROGRESSIVE SLIDE GUITAR TECHNIQUE

Progressive Slide Guitar Technique introduces you to the techniques involved in playing slide guitar. This book will be useful to modern guitar players who wish to incorporate slide into an electric rock and blues style as well as being a useful aid to guitarists who want to explore the traditional acoustic aspects of slide guitar. The types of slides available and the setting up of a slide guitar is explained. Throughout the book you learn popular slide scales, licks and solos, damping, fretting, sliding and vibrato.

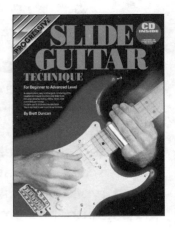

CLASSICAL

 78 Previews

PROGRESSIVE GUITAR METHOD: CLASSICAL

A comprehensive, lesson by lesson method covering all aspects of basic classical guitar technique such as proper hand techniques, progressing throught the most common keys and incorporating some of the world's most popular classical guitar pieces in solo or duet form. Music theory including the introduction of several different time signatures, open and bar chords and scales are also part of this easy to follow classical guitar method.

 79 Previews

PROGRESSIVE POPULAR CLASSICS OF THE GREAT COMPOSERS: VOLUMES 1 - 6

There has always been a need for a series of books to provide the classical guitarist with a repertoire, long available to the pianist, of the music loved by both players and listeners alike. In the *Popular Classics Series* music written by the classical greats such as Chopin, Brahms, Beethoven, Mozart etc. has been brilliantly arranged especially for the classical guitar.

 80 Previews

PROGRESSIVE FINGERPICKING CLASSICS: VOLUMES 1 - 2

The *Progressive Fingerpicking Classics Series* is designed to accommodate both classical and modern fingerstyle guitarists of all standards, through the use of standard music notation and tablature. Each piece has been thoughtfully arranged to retain the best harmonic and rhythmic intent of the original composition whilst keeping each piece as easy as possible.